This notebook belongs to:

ISBN-13: 979-8541950038

Printed in Great Britain
by Amazon

22007816R00068